Prove It!

Fact-Finding Secrets of a Fanatical Online Researcher

By Shirley Siluk

First published in 2014 by freetothink books

freetothinkbooks.com

Gulf Breeze, FL 32563

To Mom and Dad

Table of Contents

Introduction_____ 7

1. Cast a Wide Net_____ 9

2. Drill Down_____ 16

3. Locate Your Primary Sources_____ 22

4. Verify What You Find_____ 27

5. Researcher Beware_____ 34

6. When the Truth Eludes_____ 40

Bonus Chapter: Government and Organization
Resources_____ 46

Introduction

Doing research for a writing project – whether it's a breaking news story, a paper for English class or a breakthrough novel 10 years in the making – is a "best of times/worst of times"[1] proposition in today's digital era. The always-on, accessible-from-almost-anywhere internet makes it possible to find huge volumes of information quickly. At the same time, though, "huge volumes" don't help when all you need is one simple answer or one basic fact.

Even with the help of Google, winnowing down petabytes' (a petabyte is 100 million bytes) and exabytes' (one billion bytes) worth of information into the couple of sentences or paragraphs you need is a challenge. As a longtime independent journalist who's worked online since the web's early days, I've discovered lots of tips and tricks for sifting good data from bad. I've also developed a finely tuned level of skepticism that helps to alert me when something sounds "fishy."

That's more important than ever these days, when online astroturfing[2] is rampant, "sock puppets"[3] abound and everyone from your run-of-the-mill internet troll[4] to the US National Security Agency[5] is manipulating online content and electronic communications for fun, profit and other reasons.

You only have to look as far as the latest viral news story[6] to realize how quickly and easily falsehoods, half-truths, little white lies and sins of factual omission can spread and take on a life of their own. It doesn't much matter if the original publication later prints or posts a correction or clarification: the original article – often saved as a screenshot – stays out there on the interwebs forever, ready to be conjured up again and again as "proof" that something is or isn't true. Of course, just because something is online doesn't mean it's true ... but that

---

[1] http://en.wikiquote.org/wiki/A_Tale_of_Two_Cities#Chapter_I_-_The_Period
[2] http://en.wikipedia.org/wiki/Astroturfing
[3] http://en.wikipedia.org/wiki/Sockpuppet_(Internet)
[4] http://en.wikipedia.org/wiki/Troll_(Internet)
[5] http://www.theguardian.com/world/nsa
[6] http://www.bbc.com/news/blogs-echochambers-27417109

doesn't prevent a whole lot of people from trying to prove otherwise, and they can often do so quite convincingly.

That reality explains why – after decades of validated research and data-gathering by thousands of the world's leading climate scientists[7] – climate "skeptics" are still accorded equal status in he-said-she-said-type news articles and reports. It explains why people still believe weapons of mass destruction[8] were found in Iraq, and why thousands of parents choose not to have their children vaccinated[9] for easily prevented and once-again increasingly dangerous diseases. This is not just a problem of journalism or fact-checking ... misinformation can have ramifications that are literally life or death.

The bad news is that, if you're a working writer, you are 100-percent guaranteed to encounter this problem during your research and fact-checking efforts. The good news is that there are many reliable and dependable ways to help separate fact from fiction online. The truth – as the very fictional TV show The X-Files[10] taught us – is out there.

---

[7] http://cmbc.ucsd.edu/Research/Climate_Change/Oreskes 202004 Climate change.pdf

[8] http://www.gpo.gov/fdsys/search/pagedetails.action?granuleId=&packageId=GPO-DUELFERREPORT&fromBrowse=true

[9] http://www.bmj.com/content/342/bmj.c7452

[10] http://en.wikipedia.org/wiki/The_X-Files

1. Cast a Wide Net

Assuming you've just started researching a topic you don't know much about, your best way to start is by gathering a wide, broad range of general information about that subject. The go-to first stop for most of us these days is, of course, Google.

Google It

Going to Google[11] first has become second nature for most of us when we start looking for information online. It's an effective launch pad to all types of sources, but don't expect it to immediately lead you to the *right* sources ... because you tend to get millions of results for most search terms.

To fine-tune your results, try some of these tricks:

- Put your search term in quotation marks – For example, if you're looking for information about what municipal leaders around the world are doing to improve their communities, a search for "smart-city projects" will generate more focused results than will a search using that same term without the quotes.
- Add a filter term – If you're looking for a specific research document, search using the title in quotation marks along with a ".pdf" or a ".doc." That could help you more easily find the original document, rather than lots of news stories and blog posts that simply refer to the research document's title.

---

[11] https://www.google.com/

- Search Google News[12] instead of just Google – A basic Google search – for instance – might help you find a business that, according to its own website, looks super-green and eco-friendly. A Google News search, on the other hand, might help you discover links to news reports that this same business has been fined repeatedly for dumping untreated sewage in local waterways.
- Try one of Google's other specialized searches. There's Google Scholar[13] for academic papers, books and research; Google Trends[14] for seeing which search terms are currently most popular, and how interest in various search terms has evolved over time; Google Images[15], which lets you search photos, drawings and more by either URL or image file; and Google Blog Search[16], to name just a few.

Go to Wikipedia

After an initial search at Google, a visit to Wikipedia[17] can help you find a good overview of whatever it is you're researching, whether the topic is climate change or women's college basketball. The typical Wikipedia entry can provide a useful introduction to a subject you might not know much about.

Even more useful, though, are the features at the bottom of most Wikipedia entries:

- *See also* – This section provides links to other entries at Wikipedia about related topics you might or might not know about.

---

[12] https://news.google.com/
[13] http://scholar.google.com/
[14] https://www.google.com/trends/
[15] http://images.google.com/
[16] https://www.google.com/blogsearch
[17] http://en.wikipedia.org/wiki/Main_Page

- *Notes* – Information here offers further clarification about specific details in the entry.
- *References* – Items listed here can include valuable links to primary sources about the topic at hand. For instance, references for the Wikipedia entry on "methane" feature links to methane-specific research from the Intergovernmental Panel on Climate Change and peer-reviewed research articles in the journal *Science*.
- *External links* – Like the references section, this section includes links to websites and organizations with original and in-depth information about the topic at hand.

As an open-access resource, Wikipedia can be edited by pretty much anyone with an account, so it's important to remember that – while it's an extremely helpful source of information – it is not a *primary* source of information and it can feature information that is flat-out wrong. That's why, for example, teachers typically don't want their students to cite Wikipedia in their schoolwork, and why medical professionals urge people to check with their doctors[18] instead of relying on health information from Wikipedia entries. As a starting point for research, however, it can be invaluable.

Do a Snopes Check

When it comes to checking online rumors, reports of odd trends and general misinformation on the web, Snopes[19] is always a good place to visit. A quick search there can quickly tell you whether a small but growing number of cash-strapped college students are coming down with scurvy (short answer: no[20]) or whether counting cricket chirps can help you tell the temperature (yes[21]).

---

[18] http://www.bbc.com/news/health-27586356
[19] http://www.snopes.com/
[20] http://www.snopes.com/college/horrors/scurvy.asp
[21] http://www.snopes.com/science/cricket.asp

The typical Snopes entry also includes links to other sources that verify or disprove the rumor in question. These can help you find the original sources you need for a particular story or research paper.

Other Search Resources

Depending upon the type of research you need, some of the other following resources might prove handy:

- BASE (http://www.base-search.net/) – The Bielefeld Academic Search Engine, operated by Germany's Bielefeld University Library, lets you search academic, open-access documents from numerous scholarly journals and institutions.
- Directory of Open Access Journals (http://doaj.org/) – Searching content from open-access, peer-reviewed academic journals, the DOAJ aims to serve as the "one-stop shop for users of open access journals."
- Infomine (http://infomine.ucr.edu/) – A virtual library for scholarly research, compiled by librarians from the University of California, Wake Forest University and other institutions.
- IPL2 (http://ipl.org/) – Formerly the Internet Public Library; you can find more details about this one below.
- LexisWeb (http://www.lexisweb.com/) – A free search service of LexisNexis, LexisWeb is a tool for researching legal and governmental issues.
- Metasearch engines – These conduct searches of multiple search engines at once to generate the results that are most relevant to your search terms. Metasearch engines include Dogpile (http://www.dogpile.com/), Zoo (http://www.zoo.com/) (formerly MetaCrawler) and Mamma (http://www.zoo.com/).
- Wolfram|Alpha (http://www.wolframalpha.com/) – Wolfram|Alpha is a "computational knowledge engine" that uses algorithms and online information to generate

answers to questions, rather than take you to a results page full of websites that might have the answer to your question.

Example 1: War Plans for the Zombie Apocalypse

Science of Zombies[22] is one of my "fun" blogs. I'm not even much of a fan of zombie movies, but in researching an e-book for kids – *100 Cool Things about Zombies*[23] – I discovered that the zombie concept gets a lot of serious interest in the world of academia, and that some types of zombies ("zombie ants" infected by a parasite, for example) are in fact real.

To find legitimate news stories about zombie science to post on my blog, I generally go to two sites first: Google News and EurekAlert![24], a global science news service operated by the American Association for the Advancement of Science (AAAS). On one particular day, my search on Google News turned up a really promising story: numerous news reports from a variety of sources – CNN, *The Telegraph*, *The Chicago Sun-Times* and so on – about the Pentagon having an unclassified military response plan for the zombie apocalypse.

Scanning a couple of the news stories, I learned that the source that broke the story was Foreign Policy[25], a well-respected online publication first launched in print form during the Vietnam War. Going to that article, I found – at the bottom – a Scribd document and link for CONPLAN 8888, an unclassified "Counter-Zombie Dominance" plan

---

[22] http://www.scienceofzombies.com
[23] http://www.amazon.com/100-Cool-Things-about-Zombies-ebook/dp/B00G4HFD96/ref=la_B00J1FW6FW_1_4?s=books&ie=UTF8&qid=1400350373&sr=1-4
[24] http://www.eurekalert.org/
[25] http://www.foreignpolicy.com/articles/2014/05/13/exclusive_the_pentagon_has_a_plan_to_stop_the_zombie_apocalypse

created by the US Strategic Command and posted on Intellipedia[26], an online data-sharing system used by the US intelligence community. Jackpot! I had found my way to the primary source for the story.

Other Resources

Baker College Library Research Guides (http://guides.baker.edu/library) – This page lets you browse research resources on a wide variety of subjects ranging from accounting and architecture to science, speech and writing.

Directory of Open Access Journals (http://doaj.org/) – This research tool covers peer-reviewed scientific and scholarly research that is accessible without having to pay a subscription or one-time user fee.

Encyclopedia Britannica (http://www.britannica.com/) – The internet era's answer to that massive collection of print encyclopedias every kid used to research school papers back in the "dark ages" of the mid- to late 20th century.

Google Books (http://books.google.com/) – Google's book search tool also now lets users search for text in magazines as well.

Google Scholar (http://scholar.google.com/) – This is Google's search tool for academic literature, scholarly theses and court opinions.

ipl2 (http://ipl.org/) - Hosted by Drexel University's College of Information Science & Technology and a consortium of colleges and universities, this public-service resource merges collections from the Internet Public Library and the Librarians' Internet Index websites. It offers searches by subject; links to newspapers and magazines around the world; special sections for kids and teens; and special collections on US presidents, literary criticism and more.

---

[26] http://en.wikipedia.org/wiki/Intellipedia

Cast a Wide Net

Project Gutenberg (http://www.gutenberg.org/) – This site features more than 45,000 freely downloadable e-books once published in print and whose copyrights have expired. Titles include Jane Austen's *Pride and Prejudice*[27], Franz Kafka's *Metamorphosis*[28] and *Ulysses*[29] by James Joyce.

Science.gov (http://www.science.gov/) – Described as "your gateway to US federal science," this site enables searches of more than 60 databases and 2,200-plus websites from 15 federal agencies.

---

[27] http://www.gutenberg.org/ebooks/1342
[28] http://www.gutenberg.org/ebooks/5200
[29] http://www.gutenberg.org/ebooks/4300

2. Drill Down

So you've done the basics and Googled, Wikipediaed and Snoped ... now what? How can you sort the good results from the bad, and make sure the information you've found so far is based on solid, factual evidence?

Depending on the topic you're searching, the answer isn't always straightforward.

In 2012, for example, a team of US medical researchers found that fewer than half[30] (43.5 percent) of the websites found during Google searches for safe infant sleeping practices provided accurate information for parents and caregivers. Many of the results provided inaccurate information (28.1 percent) or information that wasn't relevant (28.4 percent) to the search.

The same study also found that some types of websites tended to provide accurate information more often than others. Ranked from the most to the least accurate, these types of websites included:

- Government (sites with a .gov or .state name) (80.9 percent accuracy)
- Organization (sites with a .org name) (72.6 percent)
- Company/interest group (52.4 percent)
- News site (50.9 percent)
- Sponsored links (50.7 percent)
- Educational sites (50.2 percent)
- Individuals (30.3 percent)
- Blogs (25.7 percent)
- Retail product review sites (8.5 percent)

That generally reflects my own experience as an online researcher for many years: the most reliable information and data tend to come from government and organizational sources like, for example, the US Centers

---

[30] http://www.jpeds.com/article/S0022-3476%2812%2900628-2/fulltext

for Disease Control (CDC) or the American Association for the Advancement of Science (AAAS). In the sciences, established and peer-reviewed journals – *The Lancet*[31], for instance, or *Nature*[32] – are also highly reliable sources. (It's important to note, of course, that scientific knowledge is always a work in progress. Even findings reported in the most reputable journals are sometime later corrected or even occasionally disproved.)

(For the record, while government and organizational websites tend to be reliable sources for statistics, historical data and lots of essential information, I am not suggesting that the information they provide is always accurate and/or complete. Not everything the government knows is available to the general public, nor do official pronouncements always reflect the truth, the whole truth and nothing but the truth. Just ask Daniel Ellsberg[33], who disclosed the Vietnam-Era Pentagon Papers[34], or Edward Snowden[35], who recently revealed the massive and far-reaching government surveillance of our cellphone conversations and other electronic communications.)

The guidelines above also come with another caveat: not every website is what it appears to be.

That's because it's relatively cheap and easy to create an "official-looking" website, and there are plenty of internet scoundrels who do so. Not all online scammers are sending dodgy emails from Russia or Nigeria. Some are creating websites that look like they belong to legitimate or well-known organizations. The world of online science is particularly tricky, with an explosion of what one real researcher calls "predatory" journals[36] that charge authors to publish and don't always use peer review[37] to vet research.

---

[31] http://www.thelancet.com/

[32] http://www.nature.com/

[33] http://en.wikipedia.org/wiki/Daniel_Ellsberg

[34] http://en.wikipedia.org/wiki/Pentagon_papers

[35] http://en.wikipedia.org/wiki/Edward_Snowden

[36] http://www.nytimes.com/2013/04/08/health/for-scientists-an-exploding-world-of-pseudo-academia.html

[37] http://en.wikipedia.org/wiki/Peer_review

One way to check whether an online source is legitimate is to look to the experts. University of Colorado research librarian Jeffrey Beall, for example, posts a list of "possible, potential or probable predatory open-access journals[38]" on his site, Scholarly Open Access[39]. And MacLean's columnist Julia Belluz published a helpful list of reliable health-related websites[40] on her Science-ish blog.

Because resources like these can come and go, or don't apply to other topics of research outside of science and health, there's another way to check your sources ... and that's to go back to step one and run them through Google and Google News. Chances are, if a site's a known scam, it'll likely pop up on at least a few of the results you'll get.

Another problem that can arise is when websites have similar URLs but different top-level domain designations. WhiteHouse.gov[41], for example, is the official website for the US White House, while WhiteHouse.com[42] has had a checkered past as an adult content site and WhiteHouse.org[43] was a parody site. With the continued addition of even more top-level domains[44] – everything from .finance and .dental to .vegas and .futbol – the potential for future cases of mistaken (deliberately or otherwise) identity will only grow.

See the bonus chapter at the end of this book for a list of top-level government and organization resources that can help with any information search.

---

[38] http://scholarlyoa.com/individual-journals/
[39] http://scholarlyoa.com/
[40] http://www.macleans.ca/authors/julia-belluz/a-science-ish-guide-to-self-diagnosis-on-the-web/
[41] http://www.whitehouse.gov/
[42] http://en.wikipedia.org/wiki/Whitehouse.com
[43] http://en.wikipedia.org/wiki/Whitehouse.org
[44] http://newgtlds.icann.org/en/

Example 2: Searching for Search Tools

While I'm constantly using various online search tools in my work, coming up with a comprehensive list of reliable search tools to include in this book wasn't as easy as it first seemed. A Google search for "best sites for online research" took me down more dead ends than I expected. It just goes to show, once again, how quickly things online can change.

One highly touted site that appeared in many of the results I got, for example, had morphed into a scammy looking finance webpage. A top result to an article at About.com led to one dead link after another. And some of the resources that came with great recommendations looked to me to be all but unusable.

My first rule of thumb for an online resource is, if it isn't user-friendly, intuitive and well-designed, I'm not going to even bother trying to use it. There are just too many other options out there.

Another rule of thumb is that I always prefer governmental, agency or organizational resources over commercial ones, however informative some of the latter might be. That's because the Library of Congress[45], for example, or The Royal Society[46] (a global science fellowship chartered in the 1660s) aren't likely to go away anytime soon. Plenty of online commercial ventures, on the other hand (remember GeoCities[47]?), are here today, gone tomorrow.

Ultimately, my search for the best search tools took me to a handful of sites I knew I could rely on: university-backed resources like Baker College's library research guides[48], professional/academic sites like ipl2[49] and government resources like Science.gov[50].

---

[45] http://www.loc.gov
[46] https://royalsociety.org
[47] http://en.wikipedia.org/wiki/GeoCities
[48] http://guides.baker.edu/library
[49] http://ipl.org
[50] http://www.science.gov

Other Resources

IEEE (http://www.ieee.org) – Often referred to as "I triple-E," this is the website of the professional association the Institute of Electrical and Electronics Engineers. Billed as the "world's largest professional association for the advancement of technology," the IEEE provides lots of online resources, technical articles and a digital library[51] for journalists, writers, librarians and students.

Mayo Clinic (http://www.mayoclinic.org) – A leading nonprofit in the world of medicine, the Mayo Clinic provides in-depth and reliable information on diseases and conditions, drugs, treatments and other medical issues.

National Archives (http://www.archives.gov) – Known as "the nation's record keeper," the National Archives preserves some of the most important documents related to the history of the United States. Its collection includes the Emancipation Proclamation, journals by polar explorers, treaties with native Americans, photographs from the Dust Bowl and much more: some 10 billion pages in all, along with 25 million photos and graphics, 300,000 reels of motion picture film and 133 terabytes' worth of electronic data.

National Archives for other countries (http://en.wikipedia.org/wiki/National_archives) – Wikipedia provides links and information about other national archives resources around the world, from Afghanistan to Zimbabwe.

Rhode Island College's Art and Art History Resources (http://ric.libguides.com/arthistory/) – Maintained by the college's James P. Adams Library, this resource provides links to online encyclopedias, books, online image sources and much more.

Worldometers (http://www.worldometers.info/) – This site is not only incredibly informative, but fascinating to look at as well. Run by an international team of developers, researchers and volunteers with no political, governmental or corporate affiliations, Worldometers provides

---

[51] http://ieeexplore.ieee.org/Xplore/home.jsp

Drill Down

real-time global statistics about population, public military and healthcare expenditures, number of internet users, carbon emissions, total energy used today, etc.

3. Locate Your Primary Sources

Primary sources provide information that's "straight from the horse's mouth." For instance, a BBC news article about Mars exploration is not a primary source, but a research report about that subject written by the NASA scientist interviewed for the article is.

Wherever possible, you should try to find primary sources for any information or research findings you use in your writing. That way, you can check to make sure you haven't missed anything the news articles or Wikipedia entries might have left out. The primary source also usually provides a lot more in-depth information and detail that weren't widely covered in the secondary reports. Finally, when you're using information straight from the horse's mouth, it's harder to make mistakes. You increase the odds that the only times you'll be wrong is if the horse is wrong too.

Depending upon the type of information you're researching, a primary source could include any of the following:

- Academic research papers
- Original artworks
- Autobiographies or first-person accounts
- An official government report or document
- Historical audio recordings, photos or videos
- Personal letters, emails, notes or other writings
- Collections of raw data

Your own interviews with people who can give you first-hand accounts also count as a primary source, though someone else's interview – an online Q&A, for instance – wouldn't (because you have no way of verifying how reliably that interview was conducted, recorded and edited).

These types of original information sources can be hard to find for a number of reasons: historical documents can be lost, destroyed or locked away in a hard-to-access private collection; personal writings are often closely guarded by the author or author's family; one-on-one interviews with the right people can be hard to set up; many companies and other organizations do not willingly share their raw data; and academic research papers can be protected by journals with costly paywalls. So, while you should always try to hunt down these primary sources, don't be surprised when you fall short of your goal.

When that happens, close to primary can often be good enough.

What's "close to primary"? These would be documents and online materials directly connected to the primary source. For example, if you find a research report is locked behind a paywall and can't afford to pay the fee, you might be able to get the information you need from a press release from the university at which the author works, or from the author's professional profile on the university website. You might even want to try emailing or calling the author to ask whether you could get a copy of the original research.

Primary sources, however, are always best. And locating those might occasionally require you to pay to access specialized sources or continue your research offline. As much information as there is online, not *everything* can be found online. Some answers can still be found only in original documents that haven't yet been digitized, in museum or historical society collections, in a library's rare books section ... or in the mind of a person that you'll need to interview personally.

Still, your online research will probably at least help you to identify your primary sources and track down the information you need to access them. Once you've located the necessary URLs, telephone numbers, addresses, email addresses and/or book titles, you can continue your research offline by making some calls or hitting the road.

Example 3: Living Dead Chickens

While researching the zombie war games article I described in Example 1, I learned that one of the zombie threats the US military examined in its report was chicken zombies (dubbed "CZs"). No, really.

The Conplan 8888 document stated:

"Although it sounds ridiculous, this is actually the only proven class of zombie that actually exists ... CZs were first documented in Jonathan M. Forrester's 4 Dec. 2006 online article 'Zombie Chickens Taking Over California.' "

Sensing an opportunity to write a Science of Zombies blog post about zombie chickens, I immediately looked for that article. Conplan 8888 helpfully provided a link to the article at a site called Slashfood ... but when I followed the link, I discovered Slashfood was no more and the article was gone. A Google News search of the aforementioned headline didn't work either, although it did find me a Google News scan of an article that referred to the original zombie chicken story[52].

And then I remembered the Wayback Machine[53]. A search feature on the Internet Archive[54], the Wayback Machine lets you type in any URL and find screenshots of what that URL looked like in previous years. I went there, typed in the URL from Conplan 8888 and got back results showing that page had been saved 13 times between Dec. 6, 2006, and April 1, 2008.

---

[52]

http://news.google.com/newspapers?nid=1817&dat=20061206&id=znUjAAAAIB
AJ&sjid=-acEAAAAIBAJ&pg=6693,3418625

[53] https://archive.org/web/web.php

[54] https://archive.org

Clicking the link on April 1, 2008, I found it: a screenshot of the original Slashfood article[55] by Jonathan M. Forester (one "r") about zombie chickens in California. Victory!

Other Resources

The Avalon Project (http://avalon.law.yale.edu/default.asp) - Operated by Yale Law School's Lillian Goldman Law Library, the Avalon Project archives digital documents "relevant to the fields of law, history, economics, politics, diplomacy and government." Its collections range from ancient writings from Roman statues to various drafts of the Articles of Confederation for the newly formed United States of America.

Internet Archive (https://archive.org) – Founded in 1996, the Internet Archive is a nonprofit dedicated to "building a digital library of internet sites and other cultural artifacts in digital form." It claims (as of May 2014) to have saved some *411 billion* webpages. As the example above demonstrates, this is a great resource for researching webpages that once existed but are now gone. (When you think about it, the Internet Archive's Wayback Machine is kind of a zombie webpage generator).

Quote Investigator (http://quoteinvestigator.com) – Run by a Yale PhD under the pseudonym of "Garson O'Toole," Quote Investigator features thoroughly researched articles attempting to validate or disprove the popularly held origins of famous quotes (such as, "This is not a novel to be tossed aside lightly. It should be thrown with great force[56]." Which, apparently, was coined not by Dorothy Parker but most likely by Sid Ziff, an opinionated sports columnist for *The Los Angeles Times*.)

The Straight Dope (http://www.straightdope.com/) – This site launched in 1973 as a column by Cecil Adams in the alternative news

---

55

https://web.archive.org/web/20080401112907/http:/www.slashfood.com/2006/12/04/zombie-chickens-taking-over-california

[56] http://quoteinvestigator.com/2013/03/26/great-force/

publication the *Chicago Reader*[57]. Its slogan: "Fighting Ignorance Since 1973 (It's taking longer than we thought!)" It's a great source for finding the answers to oddball questions like "Was *The Texas Chainsaw Massacre* based on a true story?[58]" (Answer: Kind of, but without Leatherface and some of the other critical details.) or "What would it cost to outfit my own pirate ship?[59]" (Answer: Around $36 million for a one-year voyage.)

JSTOR (http://www.jstor.org/) – JSTOR is a not-for-profit organization that launched a digital library in 1995. Its goal was to "help university and college libraries free up space on their shelves, save costs and provide greater levels of access to more content than ever before." Its online collection includes more than 2,000 academic journals. Many of these are available for free to anyone who registers for an online account.

AlphaGalileo (http://www.alphagalileo.org/) – Like another resource I mentioned above (EurekAlert[60]), AlphaGalileo provides news and other resources about research in science, health, technology, business, the arts, humanities and social sciences. Now an independent company supported by subscription fees and sponsorships, AlphaGalileo publishes news releases, publication announcements, and even images and multimedia resources.

---

[57] http://www.chicagoreader.com
[58] http://www.straightdope.com/columns/read/1168/was-em-the-texas-chain-saw-massacre-em-based-on-a-true-story
[59] http://www.straightdope.com/columns/read/3144/what-would-it-cost-to-outfit-my-own-pirate-ship
[60] http://www.eurekalert.org

4. Verify What You Find

Great – so you've found a reliable-looking source that appears to answer your questions. You're off to a good start, but you're nowhere near finished with your research yet.

"Reliable-looking," after all, doesn't mean "verified." And that's your next step: to find enough evidence to back up your research. The more solid evidence you have, the stronger your case will be. Even if the information you've found seems like "common knowledge," it's better to have proof.

It's like the old saying in journalism goes, "If your mother says she loves you, check it out.[61]"

There are several reasons for this kind of caution. First, because some things that "everyone" knows to be true are *not* true. Second, because wrong information online is often repeated again and again in the 'net's myriad echo chambers, making it look as if it's true just because it appears so often at so many different sources. And, third, because the deeper you dig, the more you are likely to learn. And in-depth knowledge is both rare and powerful – it will set you apart in today's shallow media world of three-second attention spans, he-said-she-said news and lowest-common-denominator native advertising[62].

The best way to verify anything, of course, is to track down the primary source. If you can find it, kudos to you. If not, though, you might learn something equally enlightening: the possibility that the "truth" is a lot more slippery than it first appears to be.

Consider this example, reported by National Public Radio's On the Media[63] program in 2010.

---

[61] http://en.wikipedia.org/wiki/Source_(journalism)

[62] http://en.wikipedia.org/wiki/Native_advertising

[63] http://www.onthemedia.org/story/132811-how-much-oil-really-spilled-from-the-exxon-valdez/transcript/

The program begins with an audio montage of news reports:

> *Female Correspondent: Twenty years ago, the Exxon Valdez spilled 11 million gallons in the water there, and fishermen say they're still healing that ...*

> *Male Correspondent: To put that in perspective for you, the Exxon Valdez spill dumped 11 million gallons of oil ...*

> *Male Correspondent: It was tremendous destructive catastrophe for Alaska, and it was only 11 million gallons of oil.*

Clearly, it had become common wisdom in the media (and in general) that the 1989 Exxon Valdez spill amounted to some 11 million gallons of oil. Only, noted the show's guest – marine toxicologist and former commercial fisherman Riki Ott – the earliest estimates given for the size of the spill when it was still happening ranged from 10.8 million to *38 million* gallons.

"Exxon never said it in a press conference," Ott said. "Just when the media started to ask questions, where did that 10.8 million gallons come from, has it been independently verified, Frank Iarossi, the owner of Exxon Shipping, at a press conference said, alcohol may be involved. And I kid you not, I witnessed the entire international media just switch tracks, and that was how we got 10.8 million gallons, rounded up to 11."

The 10.8-million-gallon figure came from a report by a contractor named Caleb Brett[64]. However, in her 2005 book, *Sound Truth and Corporate Myths: The Legacy of the Exxon Valdez Oil Spill*, Ott cites Alaska Department of Law records that indicate an independent state surveyor

---

[64] http://jlc-web.uaa.alaska.edu/client/en_US/asl/search/detailnonmodal;jsessionid=5E7C15F4371A5D47E7DB16F864492EE9?qf=AUTHOR%09Author%09Alaska.+Dept.+of+Environmental+Conservation.%09Alaska.+Dept.+of+Environmental+Conservation.&d=ent%3A%2F%2FSD_ILS%2F232%2FSD_ILS%3A232700~ILS~0~612&ps=300

believed the actual spill was much larger than reported. She also quotes an Exxon Shipping Company officer who said the remaining oil lightered (transferred) off of the stricken tanker had a high water content, suggesting much more oil escaped into Prince William Sound.

As tantalizing as these bits of information are, the dispute over the size of the Exxon Valdez spill is likely to remain unresolved. After reaching a settlement with the oil company in 1991, the State of Alaska stopped investigating the spill's volume. For better or for worse, that leaves the "official" figure for history at 11 million gallons. The whole story, however, provides a lesson in just how difficult it is to verify some facts ... and how many of the things we take at face value can prove much more complicated when you look below the surface.

It also suggests that there's probably enough doubt in the case of the Exxon Valdez for reporters to say, "at least 11 million gallons" instead of the more certain-sounding – but less verifiable – "11 million gallons."

Example 4: Hammers, Nails, Small Boys and Mark Twain

Most of us have probably heard a variation (or several) of this expression: "When the only tool you have is a hammer, everything looks like a nail." You might have even heard that this pithy saying was coined by the highly quotable Mark Twain.

The Quote Investigator[65] found otherwise.

Using Ralph Keyes' reference work "The Quote Verifier[66]" as a starting point, The Quote Investigator traced an early variant of the saying

---

[65] http://quoteinvestigator.com/2014/05/08/hammer-nail/
[66] http://www.ralphkeyes.com/quote-verifier

to an 1868 London publication called "Once a Week.[67]" That captured some of the spirit of the quote, though few of the actual words:

> *"Give a boy a hammer and chisel; show him how to use them; at once he begins to hack the doorposts, to take off the covers of shutter and window frames, until you teach him a better use for them, and how to keep his activity within bounds."*

The next iteration came from a philosophy professor named Abraham Kaplan, whose banquet speech – reported in the June 1962 edition of the "Journal of Medical Education" – included this line:

> *"Give a boy a hammer and everything he meets has to be pounded."*

Getting closer, right?

One year later, in 1963, psychologist Silvan Tomkins wrote this in a book titled "Computer Simulation of Personality: Frontier of Psychological Theory":

> *"If one has a hammer one tends to look for nails, and if one has a computer with a storage capacity, but no feelings, one is more likely to concern oneself with remembering and with problem solving than with loving and hating."*

A few years after that, another psychologist – Abraham Maslow – included this line in "The Psychology of Science: A Reconnaissance":

> *" ... I remember seeing an elaborate and complicated automatic washing machine for automobiles that did a beautiful job of washing them. But it could do only that, and everything else that got into its clutches was treated as if it were an automobile to be washed. I suppose it is tempting, if the only tool you have is a hammer, to treat everything as if it were a nail."*

---

[67] http://books.google.com/books?id=_lel8HnOA-8C&q=%22to+hack%22#v=snippet&q=%22to%20hack%22&f=false

And there you have it. Rather than being yet another witticism from Samuel Clemens (aka Twain), this aphorism came into being via a combination of expressions used by Kaplan, Tomkins and Maslow ... none of whom is as widely recognized as Twain (Maslow[68], however, is well known for his concept about the hierarchy of human needs[69].)

In his book *The Quote Verifier*, Ralph Keyes offers this logic for why some sayings are so frequently misattributed:

> *"The misattribution process is not random. Patterns can be discerned. If a comment is saintly, it must have been made by Gandhi (or Mother Teresa). If it's about honesty, Lincoln most likely said it (or Washington), about fame, Andy Warhol (or Daniel Boorstin), about courage, John Kennedy (or Ernest Hemingway). Quotations about winning had to have been made by Vince Lombardi (or Leo Durocher), malaprops by Yogi Berra (or Samuel Goldwyn). If witty, a quip must have been Twain's concoction, or Wilde's, or Shaw's, or Dorothy Parker's."*

That's a useful bit of wisdom to remember when conducting your research: Just because something "sounds right" doesn't make it so.

That quotation at the start of this chapter, by the way ("If your mother says she loves you ...")? Etymologist Barry Popik documents the earliest instances of it here[70], noting that Edward Eulenberg – one of the Chicago journalists credited with coining the phrase – "once said that his original remarks had been changed: 'What I said was, If your mother tells you she loves you, kick her smartly in the shins and make her prove it.' "

---

[68] http://maslow.org

[69] http://en.wikipedia.org/wiki/Maslow%27s_hierarchy_of_needs

[70]

http://www.barrypopik.com/index.php/new_york_city/entry/if_your_mother_says_she_loves_you_check_it_out

Other Resources

CIA World Factbook (https://www.cia.gov/library/ publications/the-world-factbook/) - The US Central Intelligence Agency's World Factbook can be a rich source of information about all 267 different countries/national entities in the world. First published in unclassified form in 1971 as the "National Basic Intelligence Factbook," the World Factbook appeared online starting in 1997. It features a wide range of data on each nation's history, people, government, geography and demographics, as well as maps, flag images, photographs and more.

FotoForensics (http://fotoforensics.com) – Encounter a photograph online that you suspect might have been altered? FotoForensics uses data and image analysis to determine whether an online photo is likely to have been modified compared to the original.

The Legal Information Institute (http://www.law.cornell.edu/) – Managed by a non-profit group at Cornell Law School, this site provides a free, open-access resource for understanding US Constitutional, federal and state law.

Newton Ask a Scientist (http://www.newton.dep.anl.gov/) – This is a great resource for out-of-the-box questions about science. Operated by Argonne National Laboratory and online since 1991, Newton enlists the help of volunteer scientists to answer questions and has assembled an archive of over 20,000 answers[71].

The OECD iLibrary (http://www.oecd-ilibrary.org) – Like the CIA World Factbook, the iLibrary is another useful source of information about the world. The online library of the Organisation for Economic Cooperation and Development (OECD) features HTML- and PDF-based publications on economic, environmental and social statistics; e-books on energy technology and policies; financial and legal journals; research papers and more.

Wikimedia Commons (http://commons.wikimedia.org/wiki/ Main_Page) – Part of the family of Wikimedia Foundation websites,

---

[71] http://www.newton.dep.anl.gov/archive.htm

Verify What You Find

Wikimedia Commons provides access to millions of images, sounds and video files that are freely usable by anyone. Some media files can be published with appropriate credit under a Creative Commons or other license, while others are public domain, which means they can be reproduced, edited and adapted without copyright restrictions.

5. Researcher Beware

As I mentioned in Chapter 2, it's pretty cheap and easy for anyone to create an "official-looking" website that isn't, in fact, official. People and organizations create sites like these for a variety of reasons, so it pays to be hyper-vigilant about the little details that separate the real from the fake: a hyphen, maybe, where the official URL does not have one, or – as in the various White House websites I described earlier – a .com domain instead of a .gov.

So who goes through the trouble of creating these troublesome online doppelgängers? Well, there are so-called "culture jammers[72]" – groups like The Yes Men that use fake sites to raise awareness about social issues and/or shame and embarrass corporations or others they believe are to blame for a problem.

One of the more infamous examples from The Yes Men – Andy Bichlbaum and Mike Bonanno – arose when they created a fake website[73] (DowEthics.com) that purported to represent Dow Chemical's stance on the deadly Bhopal gas leak[74] in 1984. Two years after they launched the site, with the 20th anniversary of the disaster approaching, Bichlbaum and Bonanno received an email request through DowEthics.com from BBC World Television asking for an interview. The duo went ahead and scheduled the interview, with one of them posing as a company spokesperson. During a live broadcast[75], the faux representative announced that Dow would accept full responsibility for the disaster and would establish a $12 billion fund for victims.

In the two hours that passed before the story was retracted, the announcement was the top item on Google News. Before the day was out, the BBC – instead of trying to make the embarrassing error go away or

---

[72] http://en.wikipedia.org/wiki/Culture_jamming

[73] http://theyesmen.org/dowtext/

[74] http://en.wikipedia.org/wiki/Bhopal_disaster

[75] http://theyesmen.org/hijinks/bbcbhopal

ignoring its mistake – wisely called back The Yes Men and conducted a followup interview about the elaborate hoax.

Other copycat and faux sites are aimed at influencing public opinion about controversial issues such as climate change, labor protection[76], gun laws, education reform, coal mining, genetically modified crops and other hot-button topics, whether local or global.

UCLA sociologist Edward T. Walker[77], who has studied the trend of manufactured "grass-roots" lobbying extensively, estimates that 40 percent of Fortune 500 companies now enlist consultants to make it look like there's a groundswell of public support for their pet issues[78]. The author of "Grassroots for Hire: Public Affairs Consultants in American Democracy[79]" (Cambridge University Press[80], 2014), Walker cites such examples as Americans Against Food Taxes (spearheaded by the soda industry) and Citizens for Tobacco Rights (led by the tobacco industry).

A similar line of research by environmental sociologist Robert J. Brulle of Drexel University found that about 75 percent of the millions of dollars supporting climate change denial now comes from "dark money[81]" (that is, sources whose identities and motivations cannot be traced). Those millions help finance, among other things, contrarian "experts" with academic titles but little expertise in actual, peer-reviewed climate science.

All this highlights the importance of being ultra-careful about which sources to believe, and which to take with a large grain of salt. As these examples illustrate, many information sources online are backed by

---

[76] http://18millionrising.org/blog/2014/may/20/gap-silencing
[77] http://www.sociology.ucla.edu/professors/Edward_T_Walker/?id=200
[78] http://www.nytimes.com/2012/08/11/opinion/grass-roots-mobilization-by-corporate-america.html
[79] http://www.edwardwalker.org/Publications.html
[80] http://www.cambridge.org/us/academic/subjects/politics-international-relations/grassroots-hire-public-affairs-consultants-american-democracy?format=PB
[81] http://www.drexel.edu/now/news-media/releases/archive/2013/December/Climate-Change/

funding to promote a particular agenda, so their take on a particular subject might be skewed or leave out facts that don't help their cause.

The bottom line is that you, as an online researcher, must always understand who or what your source is. You can't take facts, statistics or studies from any source at face value; you need to drill down and verify that the information presented is reliable, accurate and complete. How? The following strategies will help:

- Look for names behind the source – Always check the "About" page on a website to learn more about the organization behind the site. If you can't find information about the founder, board of directors or membership, be skeptical. For example, Faces of Coal[82] purports to be "an alliance of people from all walks of life" who support the coal mining industry, but its "About Us" page doesn't identify anyone in the organization and its "Our Supporters" page lists backers by first name and last initial only. A Whois search[83] by the climate-change resource DeSmogBlog[84], however, found that the website was registered to a Washington, DC-based PR firm.
- Follow the money – If a source has a financial interest in presenting a certain point of view, you need to know and check the information with other independent sources. Trade associations, for example, represent the interests of businesses in different industries, so be alert to the possibility of a pro-industry slant in the information on their websites.
- Get in touch – If you can't find the background information you need from the website, contact the organization by phone or email. No phone number, email address or contact form? That could be a red flag suggesting that the people behind the site don't want to be identified or contacted.

---

[82] http://www.facesofcoal.org

[83] http://en.wikipedia.org/wiki/Whois

[84] http://www.desmogblog.com/new-grassroots-pro-coal-group-backed-k-street-pr-firm

- Google it – By doing a Google and Google News search about a source, you should be able to track down more information about the organization's history, leadership and reliability.

Example 5: A Fruitless Search for a Smoking Gun

Remember the story in the previous chapter about how much oil actually spilled in Prince William Sound in 1989? It took me several weeks of on-and-off research to conclude that, sadly, there probably never will be an iron-clad answer to that question.

Using the Riki Ott radio show transcript as my starting point, I searched through numerous resources: The Alaska Department of Law, the Alaska Department of Environmental Conservation, the Alaska Resources Library & Information Services (ARLIS), the US Geological Survey, the Exxon Valdez Oil Spill Trustee Council. the Alaska Library Association, the US National Oceanic and Atmospheric Administration, the US Department of Transportation and archived news articles from the Anchorage Press, the Anchorage Daily News and other major newspapers. But no source provided a verifiable, alternative number for the size of the spill.

Finally, I went to Ott's website, found her email address and sent her a message asking if she could point me in the right direction. A week or so went by without an answer but – by amazing serendipity – I discovered that she would be speaking in a nearby town the following week.

So I waited, then went to her talk. After her presentation, I hung around to explain my situation. She immediately leafed through a copy of her book (I had picked up a free copy during the talk) and pointed out the passages in which she cited the independent surveyor's and shipping officer's comments. There was also a table showing estimates of how much water might have been in each of the vessels that ended up carrying away the Exxon Valdez' remaining cargo, along with a number of citations of official documents. This was great, I thought: I might actually be close to a breakthrough.

Unfortunately, my subsequent digging through all the documents didn't lead to a definitive answer. Instead, I found a number of reports that said this person or that believed differently than the official accounts … but could locate no records of actual measurements or hard data. While I found compelling reason to be skeptical of the official figure, I couldn't find any solid information to prove anything to the contrary. In other words, ample room for doubt, but no smoking gun.

Other Resources

All Acronyms (http://www.allacronyms.com/) – Every industry and field of interest has its own lingo, and it can sometimes be hard to understand what a specialist in a particular topic is talking about, especially when the acronyms start flying. All Acronyms is a great resource for identifying what exactly terms like "SOC" ("security operations center", among 500 or so other things), "ETOH" ("effective telemarketing and objection handling", and 14 other meanings) and "CIF" ("cost insurance and freight," "comment is free," etc.) stand for.

Whois (http://www.iana.org/whois) – A whois search – this one is operated by the Internet Assigned Numbers Authority – allows you to type in any URL and find out the identity of the person or organization that registered that particular website. You'll often also get other information – such as addresses, email addresses or telephone numbers – of the registered person or organization.

SourceWatch (http://www.sourcewatch.org/index.php/SourceWatch) – Published by the Center for Media and Democracy (CMD), a non-profit watchdog group, SourceWatch is an online encyclopedia "of the people, organizations and issues shaping the public agenda." It profiles front groups, industry-funded organizations, think tanks and other groups working to influence public opinion. The CMD also publishes PRWatch[85] and ALECexposed[86].

Alexa (http://www.alexa.com/) – An Amazon company, Alexa tracks internet traffic and ranks the world's top websites – globally, or by country or category. It also offers other SEO and web traffic services for a fee.

ConSource (http://consource.org/) – Established in 2005, ConSource is a free online library of documents related to the history of the US Constitution.

---

[85] http://www.prwatch.org
[86] http://www.alecexposed.org/wiki/ALEC_Exposed

6. When the Truth Eludes

Sometimes, despite your best research efforts, it will prove to be impossible to find an answer to a question. That's because not every question has an answer: some issues are still unresolved, unknown or unsettled. And some questions – how to eat healthfully, the best way to rear a child, etc. – don't *have* a single right answer. Like it or not, life is not always black and white. Gray areas are inevitable.

It's in these areas where responsible research and writing can become especially tricky.

Consider, for example, much of the news media's failure in properly covering the issue of climate change. One of the Intergovernmental Panel on Climate Change's (IPCC) most recent reports – "Climate Change 2013: The Physical Science Basis" – was released in early 2014. It is over 2,000 pages long, had more than 600 contributing authors and cites 9,200 scientific publications.

Here, now, are several essential facts:

- The latest IPCC report stated, "Warming of the climate system is unequivocal, and since the 1950s, many of the observed changes are unprecedented over decades to millennia." Look up the definition of "unequivocal," and you'll find, "leaving no doubt, unambiguous, undeniable."
- The report also stated, "It is extremely likely that human influence has been the dominant cause of the observed warming (of both the atmosphere and the ocean) since the mid-20th century." In its 2010 guidance note for "consistent treatment of uncertainties,[87]" the IPCC defined "extremely likely" as something having 95 to 100% probability.
- Finally, the report noted, "Ocean warming dominates the increase in energy stored in the climate system, accounting for more than 90% of the energy accumulated between 1971 and 2010 (high

---

[87] www.ipcc.ch/pdf/supporting-material/uncertainty-guidance-note.pdf

confidence). It is virtually certain that the upper ocean (0–700 m) warmed from 1971 to 2010 ..., and it likely warmed between the 1870s and 1971." "Virtually certain," according to the IPCC's guidance note, is defined as having a probability of 99 to 100%.

- Science historian Naomi Oreskes in 2004 examined 928 scientific papers[88] using the words "climate change" that had been published in peer-reviewed journals and found that 75% implicitly or explicitly accepted the view that human-caused ("anthropogenic") climate change was real. The other 25% were focused on methods or paleoclimate, so didn't take a position. Not one of the studies, however, disputed anthropogenic climate change.

- An even more in-depth study in 2013[89] looked at 11,944 peer-reviewed abstracts using "global climate change" or "global warming," and found that 97% of those taking a position supported the reality of human-caused climate change. The number of papers disputing anthropogenic climate change was "minuscule," the researchers reported, with "the percentage slightly decreasing over time."

So hundreds of the world's leading climate scientists and thousands of studies have concluded that there is a 99 to 100% probability the world is warming, and a 95 to 100% probability that humans are contributing to that warming ... yet major print news media outlets regularly quoted climate-change deniers[90] in stories about the IPCC's latest report. (A full half of those quoted in *The Wall Street Journal* were deniers.)

As many analysts have noted, climate change remains controversial not because it's "uncertain" or a "myth," but because of what it implies are the best solutions. A global problem like this will most likely require coordinated, global cooperation and, yes, regulation ... and that's anathema to many big-business interests and people with libertarian or free-market ideologies. When the likely cure to a problem

---

[88] http://www.sciencemag.org/content/306/5702/1686.full

[89] http://www.iopscience.iop.org/1748-9326/8/2/024024/article

[90] http://mediamatters.org/research/2013/10/10/study-media-sowed-doubt-in-coverage-of-un-clima/196387

flies in the face of everything a person believes about how things *should* work, it's entirely predictable that person will try to deny or diminish the problem itself. (As Upton Sinclair famously said, "It is difficult to get a man to understand something, when his salary depends upon his not understanding it.")

While the case for human-caused climate change is easily backed by a wealth of data (see above), other controversial topics can prove harder to tackle. That's especially true for issues people that take even more personally: childhood vaccination and perceived risks, religion's place in private and public life, choice of medical treatments, education preferences, gun control, soda taxes, etc. Facts and faith often operate in two separate spheres, and people don't always make decisions based on what's true ... or even what's best for them personally.

Journalists, writers and researchers have a responsibility to present the truth as fairly, accurately and completely as possible. This requires not shying away from "inconvenient" truths. But it also requires addressing *why* some people might consider such truths to be inconvenient, as well as what areas might remain gray or unknown.

What it *doesn't* require is spin, obfuscation, manipulation or sins of omission (as in, "Oh, this last fact completely invalidates my argument, but all these other ones support it, so I'm just going to ignore this.") Like it or not, if you've found that something is true – even if you find it unpalatable – you have to acknowledge it and deal with it responsibly.

Your readers, on the other hand, have no such obligation. So don't be surprised if, no matter how thoroughly you've researched and no matter how strong a case you make, some people attack you vociferously.

It can be frustrating to discover that, despite your most valiant efforts at well-documented and well-substantiated research, some readers will not believe you[91]. There's a growing body of scientific

---

[91]

http://www.psychologicalscience.org/index.php/publications/observer/obsonline/q-a-with-psychological-scientist-stephan-lewandowsky.html research into the reasons for this[92], as well as into the ways to best combat it[93].

It's a fascinating subject where we're learning more all the time about why there's so much cognitive dissonance[94] and misinformation out there. Scientists haven't yet found a cure for the reader who refuses to accept facts. The best approaches they've identified so far are so-called "debiasing" techniques, like repetition of key facts and explanations with a "compelling, coherent storyline."

Summing up current research on misinformation, Margaret Weigel writes in Journalist's Resource[95], "(R)etractions with the greatest chance of success acknowledge an individual's existing beliefs and offer a comprehensive alternate worldview. Persistent misinformation may respond best to 'nudging,' or introducing behavioral interventions, such as promoting low-emission vehicles even as some continue to question climate change. Perhaps the best antidote to misinformation, the authors suggest, is maintaining a skeptical attitude and an open mind."

Example 6: Freedom of Information

Public records are, well, public. And in the United States, citizens are guaranteed access to government public records under the federal Freedom of Information Act[96] and the various state public record laws[97].

92

http://www.psychologicalscience.org/index.php/publications/observer/2013/november-13/inconvenient-truth-tellers.html

[93] http://journalistsresource.org/studies/society/news-media/misinformation-correction-successful-debiasing

94

http://ageconsearch.umn.edu/bitstream/166096/2/Cognitive_Dissonance_v6_Jessica%20Cao.pdf

[95] http://journalistsresource.org/studies/society/news-media/misinformation-correction-successful-debiasing

[96] http://www.foia.gov

[97] http://www.foiadvocates.com/records.html

While the definition of a "public record[98]" can vary from place to place, among the documents that are generally available to citizens are official licensing records (such as medical, legal and business licenses), arrest records, property records (such as sales and deed transfers), government purchase and contract records, and marriage, birth and death records.

Increasingly, the internet has made it possible to access a lot of these records electronically. However, when records aren't available online, you might still be able to access them by visiting the appropriate government agency and submitting a Freedom of Information Act (or FOIA) or public records request. (Any member of the public can do this – you don't need to be a journalist – although different exceptions are in place, depending on where you're making the request.)

If your first request for information is denied, you generally have a few ways to appeal, starting with an administrative appeal and then moving on to a court appeal.

Using public records searches and requests, for example, the USA Today and Gannett newspapers[99] recently obtained documents from over 125 police agencies in 33 different states. The information in those documents revealed that many local and state police departments are using "Stingray" electronic devices to capture data from hundreds – even thousands – of cellphones at a time.

The USA Today reported, "About one in four law-enforcement agencies have used a tactic known as a 'tower dump,' which gives police data about the identity, activity and location of any phone that connects to the targeted cellphone towers over a set span of time, usually an hour or two. A typical dump covers multiple towers, and wireless providers, and can net information from thousands of phones."

---

[98] http://www.netforlawyers.com/page/how-public-are-public-records
[99] http://www.usatoday.com/story/news/nation/2013/12/08/cellphone-data-spying-nsa-police/3902809/

Other Resources

UIA IGO Search (http://www.uia.be/s/or/en/igo) – This is an incredibly powerful, free search service from the Union of International Associations. Type in a word or term here, and you can search the websites of more than 3,000 intergovernmental organizations (including the UN, European Commission, World Bank, etc.) at once.

Ballotpedia (http://ballotpedia.org/Main_Page) – This wiki-based encyclopedia provides information about US politics and elections at the local, state and federal level. It's sponsored by the non-partisan and non-profit organization, the Lucy Burns Insitute.

Cambridge Dictionaries Online (http://dictionary.cambridge.org/) – Designed for intermediate-level English learners, this online collection of dictionaries can be a useful resource for anyone. In addition to dictionaries of both British and American English, the site features a number of bilingual dictionaries, including English-Spanish, English-Chinese (simplified and traditional), English-Arabic, English-German, English-Portuguese, English-Korean, English-Italian, English-Catalan, English-Japanese, English-Polish, English-Russian, English-Turkish, and English-French.

World History Association (http://www.thewha.org/) – The website for this all-volunteer organization features a comprehensive set of links[100] for researchers looking for historical resources, from history departments around the world to region-specific research materials to other history organizations and blogs.

DMOZ (http://www.dmoz.org) – Originally called the Open Directory Project, DMOZ claims to be the "largest, most comprehensive human-edited directory of the web." It is a free, open-source site that can be edited by anyone who submits an application and is accepted by the community's senior editors.

---

[100] http://www.thewha.org/resource-links/research-links/

Bonus Chapter: Government and Organization Resources

Government/Quasi-government Resources: US

- **Army Corps of Engineers**: http://www.usace.army.mil
- **Broadcasting Board of Governors**: http://www.bbg.gov
- **Bureau of Alcohol, Tobacco, Firearms and Explosives**: http://www.atf.gov
- **Bureau of the Census**: http://www.census.gov
- **Bureau of Labor Statistics**: http://stats.bls.gov/
- **Centers for Disease Control and Prevention** (CDC): http://www.cdc.gov
- **Central Command** (CENTCOM): http://www.centcom.mil
- **Central Intelligence** Agency: http://www.cia.gov
- **Commission on Civil Rights**: http://www.usccr.gov
- **Congressional Budget Office**: http://www.cbo.gov
- **Consumer Financial Protection Bureau:** http://www.consumerfinance.gov
- **Consumer Product Safety Commission:** http://www.cspc.gov
- **Courts**: http://www.uscourts.gov
- **Customs and Border Protection:** http://www.cbp.gov
- **Department of Agriculture:** http://www.usda.gov
- **Department of Commerce**: http://www.commerce.gov
- **Department of Defense:** http://www.defense.gov
- **Department of Education:** http://www.ed.gov
- **Department of Energy:** http://www.energy.gov
- **Department of Health and Human Services:** http://www.hhs.gov
- **Department of Homeland Security:** http://www.dhs.gov
- **Department of Housing and Urban Development:** http://www.hud.gov
- **Department of the Interior:** http://interior.gov
- **Department of Justice:** http://www.justice.gov
- **Department of Labor:** http://www.dol.gov

- **Department of State:** http://www.state.gov
- **Department of Transportation:** http://www.dot.gov
- **Department of the Treasury:** http://treasury.gov
- **US Department of Veterans Affairs:** http://www.va.gov
- **Environmental Protection Agency:** http://www.epa.gov
- **Federal Aviation Administration:** http://www.faa.gov
- **Federal Bureau of Investigation:** http://www.fbi.gov
- **Federal Election Commission:** http://www.fec.gov
- **Federal Emergency Management Agency** (FEMA): http://www.fema.gov
- **Federal Highway Administration:** http://www.fhwa.dot.gov
- **Federal Reserve System:** http://www.federalreserve.gov
- **Federal Trade Commission:** http://www.ftc.gov
- **Fish and Wildlife Service:** http://www.fws.gov
- **Food and Drug Administration:** http://www.fda.gov
- **Forest Service:** http://www.fs.fed.us
- **General Services Administration:** http://www.gsa.gov
- **Geological Survey:** http://www.usgs.gov
- **Government Accountability Office:** http://www.gao.gov
- **Government Printing Office:** http://www.gpo.gov
- **House of Representatives:** http://www.house.gov
- **Immigration and Customs Enforcement:** http://www.ice.gov
- **Internal Revenue Service**: http://www.irs.gov
- **Joint Chiefs of Staffs:** http://www.jcs.mil
- **Library of Congress:** http://www.loc.gov
- **Mint:** http://www.usmint.gov
- **National Aeronautics and Space Administration:** http://www.nasa.gov
- **National Archives:** http://archives.gov
- **National Gallery of Art:** http://www.nga.gov
- **National Highway Traffic Safety Administration:** http://www.nhtsa.dot.gov
- **National Labor Relations Board:** http://www.nlrb.gov
- **National Oceanic and Atmospheric Administration** (NOAA): http://www.noaa.gov
- **National Park Service:** http://www.nps.gov
- **National Science Foundation:** http://www.nsf.gov

- **National Security Agency:** http://www.nsa.gov
- **National Transportation Safety Board:** http://www.ntsb.gov
- **Nuclear Regulatory Commission:** http://www.nrc.gov
- **Occupational Safety and Health Administration** (OSHA): http://www.osha.gov
- **Office of the Federal Register:** http://www.ofr.gov
- **Office of Management and Budget:** http://www.whitehouse.gov/omb
- **Peace Corps:** http://www.peacecorps.gov
- **Pension Benefit Guaranty Corporation** (PBGC): http://www.pbgc.gov
- **Postal Service:** http://www.usps.com
- **Secret Service:** http://www.secretservice.gov
- **Securities and Exchange Commission:** http://www.sec.gov
- **Senate:** http://www.senate.gov
- **Small Business Administration:** http://www.sba.gov
- **Smithsonian Institution:** http://www.si.edu
- **Social Security Administration:** http://www.ssa.gov
- **Supreme Court of the United States:** http://www.supremecourt.gov
- **Trade and Development Agency:** http://www.ustda.gov
- **USA.gov**, official web portal for the US government: http://www.usa.gov
- **White House:** http://www.whitehouse.gov

(For a comprehensive A-to-Z list of US government departments and agencies, go to USA.gov at http://www.usa.gov/directory/federal/index.shtml)

Government/Quasi-government/Inter-governmental/Other resources: Global

- **Academy of European Law**: http://www.era.int
- **African Union**: http://www.au.int/en/
- **American Association for the Advancement of Science**: http://www.aaas.org
- **Asian Cooperation Dialogue**: http://www.au.int/en/
- **Association of Southeast Asian Nations**: http://www.asean.org
- **British Science Association**: http://www.britishscienceassociation.org
- **The Cooperation Council for the Arab States of the Gulf**: http://www.gcc-sg.org/eng/index.html
- **European Centre for Disease Prevention and Control**: http://www.ecdc.europa.eu
- **European Commission**: http://ec.europa.eu
- **European Environment Agency**: http://www.eee.europa.eu
- **European Institute of Innovation and Technology**: http://www.eit.europa.eu
- **European Railway Agency**: http://www.era.europa.eu
- **European Space Agency**: http://www.esa.int
- **Intergovernmental Panel on Climate Change**: http://www.ipcc.ch
- **International Council for Science**: http://www.icsu.org
- **The International Monetary Fund**: http://www.imf.org
- **International Olympic Committee**: http://www.olympic.org
- **International Union for the Conservation of Nature**: http://www.iucn.org
- **Interpol**: http://www.interpol.int
- **The Nobel Foundation**: http://www.nobelprize.org
- **North Atlantic Treaty Organization**: http://www.nato.int
- **Organization of American States**: http://www.oas.org

- **Organization for Economic Co-operation and Development**: http://www.oecd.org
- **Organization of the Petroleum Exporting Countries** (OPEC): http://www.opec.org
- **Pacific Islands Forum**: http://www.forumsec.org
- **The Royal Society:** http://www.royalsociety.org
- **South Asian Association for Regional Cooperation**: http://www.saarc-sec.org
- **Union of Concerned Scientists:** http://www.ucsusa.org
- **Union of International Associations:** http://www.uia.org (free open yearbook online: http://www.uia.org/ybio/)
- **Union of South American Nations:** http://www.unasursg.org (Spanish)
- **United Nations**: http://www.un.org
- **United Nations University**: http://www.unu.edu
- **World Bank**: http://www.worldbank.org
- **World Health Organization**: http://www.who.int
- **World Meteorological Organization:** http://www.wmo.int
- **The World Nature Organization**: http://www.wno.org
- **The World Trade Organization**: http://www.wto.org

Other freetothink book titles:

100 Cool Things About Zombies (2013)

100 Ways to Make Money Online: A Guide to the 'Net's Top Freelance Marketplaces, Crowdsourcing Work Sites and Places to Sell Your Stuff (2012)

Rhythms of Shadow and Light in a Time of Divorce, Occupy and Climate Change (2012)

100 Cool Things About Bugs (2011)

For more information, visit freetothinkbooks.com

www.ingramcontent.com/pod-product-compliance
Lightning Source LLC
Chambersburg PA
CBHW060524280326
41933CB00014B/3097